Smart Password Tracker

Site	Username	Password

Smart Password Tracker

Site	Username	Password

Smart Password Tracker

Site	Username	Password

Smart Password Tracker

Site	Username	Password

Smart Password Tracker

Site	Username	Password

Smart Password Tracker

Site	Username	Password

Smart Password Tracker

Site	Username	Password

Smart Password Tracker

Site	Username	Password

Smart Password Tracker

Site	Username	Password

Smart Password Tracker

Site	Username	Password

Smart Password Tracker

Site	Username	Password

Smart Password Tracker

Site	Username	Password

Smart Password Tracker

Site	Username	Password

Smart Password Tracker

Site	Username	Password

Smart Password Tracker

Site	Username	Password

Smart Password Tracker

Site	Username	Password

Smart Password Tracker

Site	Username	Password

Smart Password Tracker

Site	Username	Password

Smart Password Tracker

Site	Username	Password

Smart Password Tracker

Site	Username	Password

Smart Password Tracker

Site	Username	Password

Smart Password Tracker

Site	Username	Password

Smart Password Tracker

Site	Username	Password

Smart Password Tracker

Site	Username	Password

Smart Password Tracker

Site	Username	Password

Smart Password Tracker

Site	Username	Password

Smart Password Tracker

Site	Username	Password

Smart Password Tracker

Site	Username	Password

Smart Password Tracker

Site	Username	Password

Smart Password Tracker

Site	Username	Password

Smart Password Tracker

Site	Username	Password

Smart Password Tracker

Site	Username	Password

Smart Password Tracker

Site	Username	Password

Smart Password Tracker

Site	Username	Password

Smart Password Tracker

Site	Username	Password

Smart Password Tracker

Site	Username	Password

Smart Password Tracker

Site	Username	Password

Smart Password Tracker

Site	Username	Password

Smart Password Tracker

Site	Username	Password

Smart Password Tracker

Site	Username	Password

Smart Password Tracker

Site	Username	Password

Smart Password Tracker

Site	Username	Password

Smart Password Tracker

Site	Username	Password

Smart Password Tracker

Site	Username	Password

Smart Password Tracker

Site	Username	Password

Smart Password Tracker

Site	Username	Password

Smart Password Tracker

Site	Username	Password

Smart Password Tracker

Site	Username	Password

Smart Password Tracker

Site	Username	Password

Smart Password Tracker

Site	Username	Password

www.ingramcontent.com/pod-product-compliance
Lightning Source LLC
Chambersburg PA
CBHW031249050326
40690CB00007B/1017
* 9 7 8 1 6 8 8 0 2 4 0 5 2 *